animal babies
in ponds and rivers

KINGFISHER

Kingfisher Publications Plc
New Penderel House
283–288 High Holborn
London WC1V 7HZ
www.kingfisherpub.com

First published by Kingfisher Publications Plc 2004
10 9 8 7 6 5 4 3 2 1

RH/0704/TWP/PICA(PICA)/150STORA

Copyright © Kingfisher Publications Plc 2004

A CIP catalogue record for this book
is available from the British Library.

0 7534 0944 5

Author and Editor: Jennifer Schofield
Designer: Joanne Brown
Picture Manager: Cee Weston-Baker
Picture Researcher: Rachael Swann
DTP Manager: Nicky Studdart
DTP Co-ordinator: Sarah Pfitzner
Senior Production Controller: Deborah Otter

Printed in Singapore

animal babies

in ponds and rivers

My body is large and my legs are short, but I can run very quickly along the riverbank.

Who is my mummy?

My mummy is
a hippopotamus
and I am her calf.

We can close our
nostrils under the
water so it
does not go
up our noses.

When I feel hungry, I plunge my head under the water to look for my food.

Who is my mummy?

My mummy is a duck and I am her duckling.

Our webbed feet help us to paddle about the pond.

I have brown fur and a short snout. When I am older, my snout will be longer and less pointy.

Who is my mummy?

My mummy is
a capybara and
I am her baby.

We need very little
sleep, so at night
we eat and swim.

I have big red eyes and I make loud, croaking noises that keep other animals awake at night.

Who is my mummy?

My mummy is a frog
and I am her baby.

We sit on lilies and wait
to 'zap' insects with our
long, sticky tongues.

I am a very good swimmer.
When it is sunny, I love
to dive, tumble and fish
in the cool water.

Who is my mummy?

My mummy is an otter
and I am her pup.

We like to play
on the muddy
banks of
the river.

My grey feathers are very soft and fluffy. When I am older, they will be snow white.

Who is my mummy?

My mummy is a swan
and I am her cygnet.

We like to sit in
our nest. It is
made from
small twigs
and reeds.

My mummy is a manatee and I am her calf.

We keep the river clean because we eat a lot of water weeds.

Additional Information

The freshwater ponds and rivers throughout the world are teeming with a great variety of plant and animal life. Some of the water animals found in this book, such as ducks, swans and hippopotamuses, live on the surface of the water, but are sometimes seen on the riverbank foraging for food, while others such as otters, capybaras and frogs live in the area surrounding rivers and ponds and spend a lot of time in the water. Manatees are found below the surface of the water.

Acknowledgements

The publisher would like to thank the following for permission to reproduce their material. Every care has been taken to trace copyright holders. However, if there have been unintentional omissions or failure to trace copyright holders, we apologise and will, if informed, endeavour to make corrections in any future edition.

Cover: Tim Davis/Getty; Half title: TJ Rich/Naturepl; Title page: Gerry Ellis/Minden Pictures; Hippopotamus 1: Daryl Balfour/Getty; Hippopotamus 2: Alissa Crandall/Corbis; Duck 1: Joe McDonald/Corbis; Duck 2: Doug Wilson/Corbis; Capybara 1: M. Watson/Ardea; Capybara 2: Francois Gohier/Ardea; Frog 1: Tim Davis/Gettyimages; Frog 2: Gail Shumway/Getty; Otter 1: Martha Holmes/Naturepl; Otter 2: Gerry Ellis/ Minden Pictures; Swan 1: TJ Rich/Naturepl; Swan 2: John Cancalosi/Ardea; Manatee 1: Brandon Cole/Corbis; Manatee 2: Douglas Faulkner/Corbis